MW00874639

Just

F*ing

Demo!

Rob Falcone

THERE WILL BE HATERS,
THERE WILL BE DOUBTERS,
AND THEN THERE WILL BE YOU
PROVING THEM WRONG.
- UNKNOWN

For my parents, family, and Liz. Thanks for riding with me
on this winding road.

CONTENTS

1 INTRODUCTION

Philadelphia, August 2010. DreamIt Ventures Demo Day. 200 investors. Hordes of media members. A quick 7 minute overview of the company I co-founded. Applause. And now... I'm told to head back to the booth and Just F*ing Demo.

I had just spent the previous 90 days with 14 other startups, frantically working to take our concepts from ideas on a whiteboard to investable companies. Everything we did, from our developers writing code to our prospective clients writing sales orders, was meant to be lean and agile. It was a truly lightning fast environment, and Demo Day, unsurprisingly, followed suit.

At Demo Day, I knew we wouldn't have much time with each investor or journalist we'd be leading demos for, but I wasn't worried. I knew my product inside and out; hell, I helped *create* the company! That's all I needed, I thought. I wasn't demo'ing intricate surgical machinery. I would just walk through why it's important and how easy it is to use, and people would get it, right?

So that's exactly what I did. I began churning through

demo after demo of our software as a service (SaaS) solution, each one unspectacularly similar to the next. I'd say hello, tell our story, and blast away with our product features; "click this then click that." Inevitably, people would seem confused or overwhelmed, politely say "thank you," and walk away.

Looking back, I realize that while *I* knew my product and what *I* wanted the demo to achieve, I had no idea what *my audience* cared about and no idea how to figure that out. Thus, I had no idea which features were most important to highlight in my demos!

Over the next few years, I diligently worked to revamp my demo skills by watching, reading, learning and rehearsing a number of different tactics. It was, admittedly, a very unscientific process filled with trial and error, and took an extremely long time. But eventually, my demos *stopped* ending with confused looks, and *started* becoming much more productive. Prospective clients were *thanking* me for being *helpful* (!) to their buying process, something every sales person hopes to hear.

Eventually, I became the top revenue-driving Solutions Engineer (the people charged with executing kickass demos) at Monetate, and implemented a training program that cut our other SEs' time to effectiveness from several months down to a matter of weeks. No more trial and error!

What was the secret? What helped me make that transition to leading kickass demos?

In short, I stopped trying to deliver the perfect demo for my **product** and starting trying to deliver the perfect demo for my **audience**. And in the coming pages, I'll walk you through some easy tactics that will help you do that.

What I hope entrepreneurs, product owners, and salespeople can take away from reading this book is that knowing your product inside and out and being able to rattle off every single feature is NOT the same as leading an effective demo.

Some of what you read in this book has been adapted from demo gurus I've learned from, and, if you have the time, I highly recommend *Demo to Win* by Robert Riefstahl, who spits a lot of excellent knowledge useful for longer, more complex sales cycles.

But the fact is, the people I'm writing this book for typically don't have months of runway to methodically figure out how to do a great demo, and are not immersed in 12-18 month sales cycles of massive systems. They're operating in agile environments similar to the startup culture I described earlier, giving virtual demos of digital apps, having conversations on conference room floors with people whose attention spans are shorter than Vanilla Ice's hip-hop career. They are the ones being pressured by prospective clients, investors, and sometimes their own colleagues to shut up and Just F*ing Demo!

Everything that follows has been written with that reality in mind; the chapters are short, and advice very tactical. To set an agenda:
- I'm going to first walk through my ideal demo structure and flow, followed by a deeper dive on some specific tactics that I use during the demo itself.
- You'll learn how to ask questions that uncover what your audience truly cares about, and how to translate that into a demo flow that is extremely easy for your audience to follow.
- My goal is that you can read this book while

drinking a few beers, *immediately* inject some of these ideas into your demos, and very quickly start to see the results.

Some caveats:

1. This book focuses on one very specific and important *component* of the sales or investment process— the demo. There is far more work to do in creating value beyond just the demo, and stacks on stacks of materials, classes, and consultants exist on the broader topic.

2. I'm focusing on the "center of mass" demo— the walkthrough of your product aimed at captivating your audience to the point where they want more. There is also a place for more nuanced demos for end users, what I call "button pushing demos," where you will go into far more depth, and where most product owners excel naturally.

3. Remember, I'm trying to save you time and get you to a great demo faster, by stripping away as much BS as possible. I want you to be able to read this book, and immediately take action.

2 'HELP' SET A GREAT AGENDA:
YOU – THEY – YOU

Shameless confession: I love food reality shows; no regrets. Watch a few food reality shows, and you'll almost certainly see an intro previewing what you'll watch on that specific episode; something like, "Tonight on *Bar Rescue*, Taffer goes batshit crazy!" These previews give away just a little bit of the content, set the expectation for what material will be covered, and give you a reason to keep watching.

"Hell yes, I want to see Jon Taffer fire undercooked chicken at an amateur chef!"

A good agenda is the key to all good product demos for the exact same reason.

You need to let your audience know where you are going to lead them, what you will cover and when. This helps prevent ill-timed questions and makes the demo immensely easier for your audience to follow. A good agenda is an incredible weapon, and an asset for even the most informal demos.

Notice that the title of this chapter is "HELP" set a great agenda. This is because you want the agenda to feel like it is customized to the audience, designed to help THEM get what THEY need from the demo, without leaving it entirely open to them.

Giving a good demo requires successfully navigating what I call the YOU – THEY – YOU approach. You are leading them down the path of [what **YOU** need to cover] as it relates to [what **THEY** say they need to learn] so that [**YOU** get what you want].

In the ideal scenario, you'll know exactly what the audience wants to achieve during the demo. For example, you head into a demo for a potential client, knowing they are looking to learn how your product can cut down the amount of IT involvement needed to push content to the website. Let's fit this short agenda statement into the YOU – THEY – YOU approach:

- YOU: I want to hit on the specific tool in our suite *we designed to help our clients push content without IT*
- THEY: So you can *learn how you could potentially cut down IT involvement in your content releases*
- YOU: So that I can *set up a much more in-depth demo with your potential end users.*

Now, let's see how the structure could drive a quick agenda statement in the "real world":

John, I know you wanted to understand how you could potentially cut down IT involvement in your content releases. Therefore, what I'll cover first today is our implementation, so you understand how we'll fit into your existing content management system. Then, I'll spend most of our time showing the specific tool in our suite we designed to help our clients push content without IT. If you like what you see, we can set up a much more in depth demo with your potential end users. Is there anything else you want to make sure we cover today?

It's important to note, in the YOU – THEY – YOU scenario I've outlined, the THEY is far and away the most important. If THEY don't learn what they want or need from the demo, then YOU will not achieve your goal. Period.

Now, let's assume I DID NOT know anything about what this person wanted to learn, and I'm being pressured to Just F*ing Demo! Should I just jump right into the product? HELL NO. It's time for The 5 Minute Discovery.

CHAPTER ACTION ITEMS
Even the most informal, on-the-fly demos begin with a strong agenda. Begin every demo with a quick agenda, and be sure to confirm that the agenda aligns with what the audience wants to learn.

3 THE 5 MINUTE DISCOVERY

Let's pretend I walk into a high-end bar and craft beer brewery, sit down at the bar, and ask the bartender for a recommendation. He could spend the next few breaths telling me about the heaviest and most delicious beer on the menu, hailed by enthusiasts as a truly decadent creation. He could tell me about hops, foam, finish, and aftertaste, even the city where the beer was brewed. It's the signature beer "everyone" asks for; he should point me there, right?

Instead, however, he responds with a *question*, and after a few minutes of dialogue, he learns that I'm actually looking for something light and cheap, and, in fact, generally never drink heavy beers. You can dress me up, but can't take me out.

This exchange underscores the most important component of YOU – THEY – YOU from the last chapter. Before determining what YOU are going to demo or what YOU want from the conversation, you first need to uncover what THEY care about.

A lot of times, you're going to feel like this bartender:

Someone is going to show up and you're going to know nothing about them. And you're going to have to rely on a small window of time to determine the most critical pieces of background information you can use to begin navigating your demo, through which you can continue to build value.

I call this The 5 Minute Discovery, which consists of asking questions that get you these **critical** pieces of information:

- **Present:** What are the challenges they've been facing?
- **Future:** What are the outcomes they are looking to drive?
- **Preference:** Do they have any specific requirements on how they get there? How do they judge the effectiveness of a solution for delivering on those?

Go back to the bar scenario above, and imagine just how the bartender could have quickly discovered the necessary information to recommend MY (not THE) ideal beer for the evening:

- **Agenda (Don't forget!):** *I'd be happy to make a beer recommendation for you. First, I typically ask a few questions to learn what types of drinks you're into and what type of night you're looking for, then I'll dive into one that I think is best. Anything else beside beer you'd like me to recommend?*
- **Present:** *Tell me what you had for dinner tonight? Typically that plays an important part in what folks elect to drink.*
- **Future:** *Talk about what type of evening are you looking for? Something laid back or are you looking to go dancing?*
- **Preference:** *Describe the types of beers you normally drink? I imagine you base your decisions on taste, hoppiness, and calorie count?*

To make this even more concrete, let's step out of the bar and re-run the scenario from the last chapter, and assume John, our prospect, called me out of the blue and asked for a demo of our tool (used to push content to the website):

- **Agenda (Don't forget!)**: *I'd be happy to walk you through our product. First, I typically ask a few questions to learn what features are going to be most important. Then, I'll walk through a few of them for you, and, if you like what you see, we can set up a more custom demo. Is there anything more specific you'd like to learn today?*

- **Present**: *How do you guys push content to the website today? How long does that generally take? Who needs to be involved today?*

- **Future**: *Is there a benchmark for how quickly you want to be able to do this in the future? What would the impact be to the business? What KPIs are you looking to drive?*

- **Preference**: *Who do you want to be involved? Are you typically more of a DIY shop or do you prefer to lean on partners for these types of projects? Where on the site would you like to push new content? How do you measure the effectiveness of tools that you use today?*

For founders, the same process can be useful for investor demos as well.

- **Present**: *What types of companies do you typically invest in? Describe some of the commonalities.*

- **Future**: *Are there specific holes in your portfolio you are looking to fill? Are there companies within your portfolio who might be looking to partner with [insert characteristic of your company]?*

- **Preference**: *Are you interested in learning a bit more about the technology behind our product, or how potential clients would utilize it? How do you evaluate scalability of a given company?*

The more of the above information you can learn in advance of your discussion, the better. It will allow your questions to be even more pointed. Using the investor example, imagine you had some advance intel on the investor you're speaking to:

- **Present**: *I noticed that [Companies X, Y, and Z] are part of your portfolio. What were some of the drivers that made them attractive when you decided to invest?*

- **Future**: *Are there specific holes in your portfolio you are looking to fill? For example, has [Company X] considered a [insert need your company fills] partner?*

- **Preference**: *I know your background is on the technical side, would you prefer if I spent a bit of extra time on the technology behind our product, or on how potential clients would utilize it?*

Remember, five minutes of discovery can be enough to get you a great first step (rather than never getting out of the starting gate) but it's NOT enough. You will need to gather more information, specifically on the pain points the audience is looking to solve and the economic value of doing so, over the coming days/weeks/months of your the race to win the deal.

CHAPTER ACTION ITEMS

No amount of product information will overcome not knowing what the audience cares about. Even if you can only squeeze in 5 minutes of questions (Present – Future – Preference) before diving into a demo, do it!

4 FAST FORWARD TO THE OUTCOMES YOU CREATE

Anyone interested in your product is not interested because of your state of the art features; they're interested because of the *outcome* it creates. It's a simple rule of buyer motivation.

Consider the worldwide sneaker revolution led by Michael Jordan. A massive movement of consumers were not clamoring for Air Jordans because of the shoes themselves—the luxurious leather, the art-inspired design, the impressive construction. No, people bought those shoes so they could look cool, they could be exclusive, and they could soar through the air like never before.

Nike had sold them on a vision of what life could be like with those kicks on their feet. *Be Like Mike.*

Which is exactly why I begin my demos at the end. You can show, in stark contrast, the outcomes (the challenge/solution or goal/accomplishments) that your product makes possible. Doing so helps frame the conversation, getting the audience to agree that, "Yes, that is what we want, but now show me how does your product make that possible?"

Discovery is key here, because, of course, you need to know the outcome that the audience is looking for. Let's pick up from the discovery we were doing with John, who is looking to push content to the website:

John, let's start the demo here, with your existing website. It's very well designed, but relatively static due to those IT challenges you mentioned earlier, is that accurate? Ok great. Now, let's take a look at how the site could look if you had our platform in your hands. You'll notice the updated pieces of real estate that you mentioned you wanted to change, and what's special is that, as you mentioned you wanted, each of these pieces of content can be manipulated without bothering your IT team, which, as you mentioned, could result in higher conversion rates with decreased internal IT costs. Before we hop into the platform itself, tell me how this aligns with what you envisioned.

A couple of specific callouts here:
- **Challenge**: *It's very well designed but relatively static*
- **Discovery - Past***: Due to those IT challenges you mentioned earlier*
- **Solution**: *Now, let's take a look at how the site could look if you had our platform in your hands*
- **Discovery – Preference**: *You'll notice the updated pieces of real estate that you mentioned you wanted to change, and what's special is that, as you mentioned you wanted, each of these pieces of content can be manipulated without bothering your IT team*
- **Discovery – Future**: *Which, as you mentioned, could result in higher conversion rates with decreased internal IT costs*

We've now set the stage to transition into showing the

audience how our platform can enable them to create the outcome you just showed. Finally! Now it's time to get into the tool/platform/user interface that you know so well, that your audience has come to see. So, is it time to put on our "user" hat and show the audience *exactly* how one would use our product? Step 1...Step 2...Step 3...Step 45...Sleep? NO.

CHAPTER ACTION ITEMS

Begin your demo by highlighting the outcomes it creates. This aligns with your audience's needs and understanding, and will frame up HOW your solution can help them create the given outcome.

5 MACRO TO MICRO: DEMO USING IMAGINARY BUCKETS

Imagine you go to a hardware store and buy a set of buckets in a nice, compact package. You take them home, open the package and start unloading your buckets, arranging them from largest to smallest (clearly a very normal activity, by the way).

This is how I conduct product demos!

Remember, YOU – THEY – YOU. YOU need to show your audience only the features they need to see, so that THEY learn what they need to. The THEY is the single most important piece of leading a great demo, and why The 5 Minute Discovery is so immensely important.

Your product, which you know inside and out, is entirely foreign to the audience. So, you need to take great care in being very deliberate about letting them know what you are showing, and why it matters based on what THEY care about.

This is where your imaginary buckets come into play. Start with what you learned in The 5 Minute Discovery. Pick out only the features of your product that would help solve the problems you learned in discovery and put them into the imaginary buckets, with the high level features going into the largest bucket, and the more nuanced features being placed in the smaller buckets.

A helpful hint: All of your product's features will not fit into your imaginary buckets, so choose only those that align with what the audience cares about. This again underscores how critical The 5 Minute Discovery is; without it, you are simply guessing on what features to put into the buckets.

Now, arrange your buckets starting with the largest bucket then the additional buckets, getting smaller and smaller. Your demo is simply a walk through the contents of each bucket.

As you arrive at each bucket, you will:
- Tell the audience what is in the bucket you are about to show them
- Show them the contents of the bucket
- Summarize why you put the contents in the bucket for them[1]

Let's walk through an (intentionally abbreviated) example using two buckets.

Bucket 1: Macro
- *First I'm going to show you our user dashboard.*

---

[1] My bucket concept is an adaptation of the "Tell – Show – Tell" tactic outlined in detail in *Demo to Win* by Robert Riefstahl.

- *On this dashboard, everything you need to push content and see KPI performance at a glance is right here.*
- *Since you mentioned having the power to push content without IT was important to you, I wanted to start here, because our platform has been ranked the #1 most user-friendly in our space.*

Bucket 2: Micro

- *Next, I want to dive into a more nuanced feature, which allows you to call out where on site you would like to push content.*
- *This feature allows you to easily mouse around the page and select exactly where your content should go.*
- *I know you're looking for customization of where content should be pushed, while also striving for time and cost savings, which is precisely what you are going to get by using this feature.*

The buckets become the backbone for your demo, and will do wonders for the amount of material your audience comprehends and remembers. They can also be moved, changed, or augmented. For example, if during the agenda your audience asks you to cover something you hadn't planned on, put it in a new bucket, and slide that bucket wherever you feel it will make the most sense.

We'll refer back to the buckets in the Demo Tactics chapter.

CHAPTER ACTION ITEMS

Plan out your demo by putting features that align with your audience's needs into "buckets". Starting with broad features and getting more nuanced, move from bucket to bucket, and for each: 1. Summarize what is in the bucket 2. Show the features 3. Summarize why the audience should care.

6 LET'S GET IN THE WEEDS:
DEMO TACTICS

Now that we've covered how to structure a demo, it's necessary to really get into the weeds and touch on a few key tactics you'll want to use. I'll get right to the point and make these as concise as possible, so you can start implementing today!

Clock Management

I've led effective demos where I've had anywhere from 10 minutes to two hours to convey why my product could help the audience create the outcomes they are looking for.

A key here is clock management; understand the YOU – THEY – YOU and how much time you have to accomplish it. If you feel like you need to speak REALLY REALLY REALLY FAST BECAUSE THE CLOCK IS TICKING…then how effectively are THEY going to learn what they need from your demo?

Instead, manage the time during your demo by shifting and removing buckets. Your audience will have a far greater comprehension of the buckets you do cover, and you can always set up a follow-up demo (in many cases, this will be your goal anyway!) to cover the buckets you missed.

Questions = Your Not So Secret Weapon

Great demos are **conversations** that uncover the audience's challenges and goals, and highlight how your product can help achieve them.

Thus, as you walk through your demo, it is incredibly important to engage your audience, so that the demo does not become a boring lecture; a great way to do this is by asking questions throughout the demo.

I typically use three types of questions in my demos:

Open-ended questions that get the audience talking:
- *What you just saw is how you could use our point-and-click interface to carve out those specific site locations to push content into. How much time would this process save versus the one you guys have in place today?*

Point questions to maximize effect:
- *What you just saw is how you could use our point-and-click interface to carve out those specific site locations to push content into. From speaking with your colleague, it seems that you guys do not have this ability today, is that accurate? And your team feels it is costing you time and money?*

Response questions (when the audience asks you a question):
- *Audience Question: Can I select the specific site locations on site where I'd like to push content?*
- *Response Question: Well, tell me, are there specific locations you'd like to push content to? What are they?*

How do you do that today? Ideally who on your team would you like to be able to do that?

The third category is extremely difficult, and the questions you ask obviously are very specific to your product. But, resist the urge to answer that question directly, unless you absolutely have to, or the question is straightforward. The information that you glean will allow your answer to be more pointed, and can allow you to avoid traps set by your competitors, or skeptical audiences.

Minimize Clicks

You are an expert at your product; to you, features that are complex probably appear straightforward. To your audience, features that are complex appear...complex and overwhelming. This problem can be exacerbated if I am click-click-clicking from screen to screen.

As such, I use a few tricks to keep the audience focused on what is most important rather than how I got there, is by:

- Pre-loading screens that take multiple clicks to reach
- Using the pause button (if doing a virtual demo)
- If I need to load a new screen, speaking directly to the audience while I do so

We vs. You

People aren't interested in your product because of what it can do; they are interested in what they can do with it. Talk about your product in that way.

Don't say things like:

- *We can ...*
- *This feature will ...*
- *What our product does here is...*

Instead, walk through your demo showcasing how your audience can use it to create their desired outcomes, with words such as:

- *Using our product, you can…*
- *This feature will allow you to…*
- *You would simply…*
- *Our current clients achieve this by…*

Here's an example, based on a recent product demo I've heard:

- *We can take the data, and display it in X ways.*
- *Then, we can update the data in real-time and output it to Y system.*

Demos with a lot of "WE's" often result in a lot of "meh" from the audience. "I get it, it looks really cool, but it seems like a lot for us to take on."

Now, take the example above, swap we for you, and use the bucket concept:

- *I'm going to walk you through the reporting capabilities of our system.*
- *You can analyze the data in these X ways in our system, which will allow you to gauge success without switching platforms.*
- *Alternatively, the data updates in real-time, and can be sent to Y system, so you can analyze it there.*
- *As a result, you'll have the flexibility get a quick look when you want it, but also dive much deeper in your legacy systems when you need to.*

If people seem to be responding to your demos with concerns around usability, have a spotter listen in on your demo, and note every time the word "WE" is used when talking about your product. Go back, and replace with YOU, and note the results.

Use Their Vernacular

Remember, you want people focusing on the key

points of your product, not distractions.

One such distraction you can eliminate is the "synonym distraction," where you and your audience might be using different words to describe the same problem or feature. As such, ALWAYS note their preferred wording, and use that throughout the rest of the demo. Your audience will now spend less time trying to figure out your lexicon, and more time on the demo.

Competitive Differentiation
In nearly every demo, you will be asked "How are you guys different than [insert competitor]." You could spend 10 minutes rambling about all of the different bells and whistles you do and they don't have, but the audience won't remember that.

Likewise, you could spend 10 minutes telling them all of the things your competitor can't do, but if you are wrong about one, your credibility is shot and you risk confrontation with your audience.

When attempting to competitively differentiate, always go back to the THEY in YOU – THEY – YOU. What does this audience value? What have you learned in discovery, and throughout the course of your demo, about what this audience truly cares about?

I try to keep as up to tabs as possible on my competitors and my industry, so that when the question arises, I can first respond with *"What I've heard from folks in the market is that the main difference between us is [insert difference]";* in spelling out the differences, I'll pivot back to the components of my product that:
- Create the outcomes the audience is looking for
- Which are truly differentiated from the competition
- Which I can back up with proof in the form of

references or case studies
- Which I can use to start asking trap setting questions about my competitors in these same areas.

You Lead "Their" Agenda

You've helped the audience create an agenda, based around what THEY are looking to learn.

Now, as questions and additional features begin to sprout up during the demo itself, ask yourself if spending time on this is going to help get the audience what they said they needed to learn. If the answer is yes, then either add these additional components into your existing buckets or into new buckets, and cover them at the appropriate time. If the answer is no, ask the audience permission to cover that material in a subsequent demo, in the name of helping them achieve their goal for the demo.

Write it Down

Simple as it seems, lost in the shuffle of many demos is the need to write things down. Do it, and let your audience know you are doing it. There are a few strategic reasons for doing this. First, and most important, writing down something that the audience says shows that you are listening and that you truly care about what they had to say.[2]

---

[2] This is another tactic covered in detail in *Demo to Win* by Robert Riefstahl, as well as in *Great Demo!: How to Create and Execute Stunning Software Demonstrations* by Peter Cohan.

The more practical reason, at least for me, to write things down is that many of the tactics I've mentioned throughout this book (YOU – THEY – YOU, The 5 Minute Discovery, Demo Buckets, Using Their Vernacular), I simply can't execute by memory alone!

Awkward Silence

In most organizations, the quiet, reserved folks are not the ones on the front lines leading product demos. Quite the contrary…we are the people who like to talk! One of the negative outcomes of this great character trait, however, is that we sometimes miss information. As such, I make it a point to leave a beat of silence after my audience finishes speaking.

Yes, it will feel unnatural at first, but allowing for a bit of awkward silence will:
- Many times, lead the audience to continue speaking, giving you more valuable information
- Give you the ability to write down any additional information
- Allow you to think, and deliver a very strategic response

CHAPTER ACTION ITEMS

These are specific tricks and tactics you can sprinkle throughout your demo to maximize your chances of success. Above all else, remember that the best demos are backdrops for a conversation about your audience's goals, and how your product can help them be achieved.

7 CLOSING THE DEMO

When I first started demo'ing, I'd end nearly every demo with three very dangerous words: "*Any other questions?*"

"*Uh, yeah, I thought we were going to talk about [insert product feature]*" might be the response from an audience where I failed to set an agenda. Alternatively, I could get "*Yeah, go back to Step 24 and walk me through exactly how that one little widget works*" from someone who didn't have the benefit of a clean bucket demo. Perhaps the worst, "*Nope, I'm good, thank you, goodbye*" would be the response from someone with whom I did no discovery and showed irrelevant features.

You've seen how the previous chapters could help mitigate each of these scenarios. So, what's the "right" way to close a demo?

Closing the demo is a very tricky subject, and very much depends on who you are talking to, where you are in a given deal cycle, and your specific role. For example, a quota-carrying sales professional speaking to a CXO might close the demo by summarizing the economic benefit of a partnership, while a sales engineer speaking to a tactical buyer might hit on required capabilities.

Remember, in the demo, you led the audience down the path of [what **YOU** needed to cover] as it relates to [what **THEY** say they needed to learn] so that [**YOU** get what you want]. Thus, I'll close the demo by:

- **YOU**: Quickly summarizing what you showed
- **THEY**: Asking if they learned what they needed
- **YOU**: Suggesting the next step

Returning to our example case, let's close this demo by summarizing the YOU – THEY – YOU.

- **YOU**: *We covered a lot in this demo, starting with a look at the content areas you'd like to change on your site, the main dashboard that is going to give you a look at all of your activity, and, finally, the content tool that will allow you to select those pieces of real estate on your site where you wanted to update content.*
- **THEY**: *You wanted to learn how your team could do all of this without IT involvement. Tell me how I've done, and where you still have questions?*
- **YOU**: *Excellent. What I'd recommend then is we set up a second, more custom demo to address those specific use cases. Is that ok?*

Note that the way the audience responds to the THEY question will tell you a ton, perhaps more than the words they say.

When I first started, I'd take the words at face value; now, I look for hesitation ("I really like it, but…"), I look for excitement ("This is exactly what I've been looking for!"), I look for confusion ("Um, yeah this, uh, makes sense.")… and then I'm ready to pounce.

Regardless of what they say, if someone is hesitant or confused, follow up with questions to figure out why. Likewise, if someone seems extremely excited, determine if you (or your teammate) should follow up with additional questions to start tying economic value to that excitement.

CHAPTER ACTION ITEMS

To close a demo, simply go back to the YOU – THEY – YOU, summarize each component and collaborate with the audience on mutually beneficial next step.

8 LOVE WHAT YOU DO

Disclaimer: I'm about to break from my "straight and to the point" M.O. for some fluff, because I think it's important.

I recently spent a few days in Napa Valley for my honeymoon, where I thought I'd walk around, see some grapes, and drink some wine. When our tour guide picked us up, she greeted us warmly, laid out an awesome agenda after she'd ask us some questions to determine which wineries to recommend (The 5 Minute Discovery!), but then she said something I felt was incredibly powerful. She said, "Ask me anything you'd like. I probably know the answer. I'm really good at what I do, because I love what I do."

You will never be great if you show up simply to Just F*ing Demo. At the end of the day, it's no secret that you're leading a product demo to secure an investment, to win a new deal, woo a new employee, impress a media outlet…whatever.

But do not underestimate how much better your demo could be if you truly LOVE the craft. This love will manifest itself, not only in your level of preparation and detail, but in subtle ways, such as smiling while speaking to the audience or getting excited over a feature that would help them achieve their goals.

People are buying the outcome your product creates, but they are also very much buying YOU.

So whether it's because you are the founder of the product that you poured your blood, sweat, and tears into, or a seasoned sales person who just enjoys chasing the deal, figure out what you love, and then...Just F*ing Demo.

SHOUT OUTS

My journey has certainly been a winding one, and I'm incredibly fortunate that some amazing people helped me find my way. I have the opportunity to do something I love day in and day out thanks to your support, guidance, encouragement and willingness to join me on my journey. This book is simply the latest example.

First, thanks to Leo Strupczewski for jumping on board with this project, and sharing with me your incredible gift of turning *words* into *meaning*.

Drexel Athletics and the DAC Pack gave me an outlet to discover that electrical engineering was not for me, but that sales and marketing certainly was. I'm eternally grateful for allowing me to take the first steps toward my true calling.

David Bookspan and the partners at DreamIt Ventures have been incredible mentors, and truly do live by their belief in the value of investing in *people*. Thank you for saying 'yes' and helping me go places I truly never imagined I would.

I'm extremely grateful to be a part of the team at Monetate. The ability to continue developing my passion for sales and marketing would not have been possible without the company's unwavering belief in cross-functional collaboration and personal growth.

To my Philly / Drexel guys (you know who you are) who have always been my biggest cheerleaders and have made me feel like I could do *anything* I worked hard for - you don't know how much you mean to me.

My wife Liz has been my partner, confidant, sounding board and co-pilot as I've navigated this winding road; I certainly wouldn't have had the bravery to continue searching for my calling if not for your love and support. I love you so much.

Lastly, to my parents and family: you've always known when to give me a pat on the back as well as a kick in the ass. From my earliest days as a fifteen-year-old selling sunglasses, to the decision to write this book today, you've pushed me to never take no for an answer and to always challenge myself. I'm so lucky to have you in my corner.

ABOUT THE AUTHOR

Rob Falcone helps some of the world's leading brands accelerate digital revenue growth by delivering optimization and personalization tactics to their marketing teams. He is a President's Club winning seller, who currently leads a team of digital marketing experts spanning Philadelphia, Chicago, and San Francisco.

Prior to joining Monetate, he co-founded an award winning social media startup that was selected for funding by DreamIt Ventures, one of the world's top 15 startup accelerators.

Rob earned his MBA from Drexel University in Philadelphia.

Made in United States
North Haven, CT
25 September 2022

24542391R00026